Copyright

To my parents, for always pushing me and knowing I was capable even when I didn't.

To my brother, for listening to my listless rambling.

To my family for always believing in me.

To my friends, some of whom have already read these more times than I can count.

And to you, reader. I hope you find some comfort here.

Take a breath.

Contents

I want to paint myself in colours that will never fade.

(everyone deserves to be remembered)

'Ghosts can't love.'
What kind of ghost?
The dead or the living?
The empty shells or those at rest?
Because only one of them can see the
flicker of candles
And not wish to be draped in a pall of
their own design.

'Ghosts can't love.'
Because they're here or because they
aren't?
Many worship a God who defies all laws of
space and time
While they can forget about the person
Selling their souls two feet away to make
sure they're ok.
Is He the exception, or the rule?

'Ghosts can't love.'
Except some can.
The ones far away enough to understand
That loving someone doesn't require
peace
That love is an abstract masterpiece
One every living should live to see

Even the ghosts who can't love
Who wield fire in an attempt to warn off
the cold
Not noticing the forest they destroyed
In an attempt to fill that void.

But what about you?
Are you at peace enough
To love a ghost
Who couldn't possibly love you?

(ghosts are just as alive as us)

You always come back.
That's why I can never quit you.
You always know exactly what to say
And I think that's why I welcome you home
To a home you have no idea belongs to you.
To be clear, this is not a love poem
You do not own my heart
Just a little piece of my mind
With your stupid
Offerings and extended hands
When I confess I want to bear my soul to you
And don't get me started on
You meeting my fleeting optimism
That one day our paths will cross
By staking your belief in the universe on it
This is not a love poem.
I am not in love with you
And you are not in love with me.
Who knows, maybe in another life we would be.
But we aren't.
But we can't.

But we won't.
The sinking feeling in my stomach
When you forget I exist
Is a fear you never did.
I would nurse your wounds
A million times over
If you would just forget me a little less.
Bullet holes were not designed for heroes
But I was never much of a hero
So what's one bullet hole more?

(people were not made to be bulletproof)

Promise me that if I die before you, you'll remember me as fearless in all the ways that matter.

(there's more than one way to face your fears)

I'll learn how to stand up for myself someday, but today could I stand up for you?

(i never was good at putting myself first)

Gladiator in arena consilium capit.
The gladiator is formulating her plan in
the arena.
She will not stand silently by
As a witness to the carnage.
She will not let them fade quietly into the
night
Her rage will burn no less bright.
She is prepared to don her armour
And if it is to be a battle to the death
Then so be it
She will bring death
To Death's door.
She burns
With the rage
Of a thousand injustices
A million failures
A storm in skin
Is oh so much harder to restrain
Than a cloaked figure
Clutching a bloodstained scythe.
Gladiator in consilium capit.
She is coming.
And she has brought hell with her.

(freedom should not have to be fought for)

This is to the boys
The boys who think
My life is a privilege
Which they are owed
To the boys
Whose hands have roamed
To places that should have left them
With nothing
To the boys
Who hear a million melodies
In a single word

Do you think our tears
Taste sweet
When they run to our mouths
The way we wish
Our voices would?

Do you think our fists
Shake
With excitement?

Do you think our hearts
Will miraculously forgive you
And our brains
Will offer an open invitation

Next time?

We do not owe you ourselves
In the way you owe us peace
For now we are stood
In a gallery
Of ripped masterpieces
Each with a corner missing

One day they will form
A patchwork hall
So bright and powerful
You will fall to your knees
Begging for reprieve
Trying
And failing
To explain
Your belief
That we wanted it
That you didn't owe us dignity
And you will weep
While the walls heave
With the weight
Of our long repressed sighs

You see

We don't owe you forgiveness
And you taught us kindness doesn't come
for free
So the only person I will ever owe
Is the girl I used to be

(we will heal on our own terms)

You're scared of me now
Of who I could have become
But like I explained to her
A girl who can put herself back together
Doesn't need a gun.

(i am not as weak as you think)

I'm busy grieving all the people I could have been.

(how many funerals can you have for one person?)

Do we get a choice?
We're born
And named
And raised
Without our permission
We're put on a path
That our parents wished they had
walked
And set up
To continue the cycle
Of living our lives
A generation behind
Growing
A generational divide
Who of us
Would have been
Dreamers
Wanderers
Pucks
Instead of
Lawyers
And doctors
And athletes?
Who let them choose
To take away our choice?
Who handed them the reins

And the whips
To allow them
To force us
Down the straight and narrow
Rather than gifting us a map
So we can find new ways
Through concrete jungles
Instead of a guided ghost tour.
You wish they had listened to you.
Why are you making us
Live through this nightmare too?

(they don't owe you their futures)

London is a beauty
The world has always seen
And yet I found my place
Beside a fallen tree

(we were made for different places)

I want to wake up early
And drink my coffee
While the sun wakes
Oh, so slowly
It's warm fingers
Caressing the pages of my favourite
book.

I want to wander sleepy streets
And feel
Mystery trailing in my wake
Treading lightly in the footsteps
Of those before me
In a place I will never be again.

I want to swim
In every ocean
And be among
A simpler type of beauty
Where freedom
Is endless.

I want to know
That although fractured
The world is still whole
And as brave as it would be

To be the last one standing
I'd rather not stand alone.

(dream yourself a kinder future)

Alpha centauri a
And
Alpha centauri b
Only orbit each other every 80 years
But are still inexplicably linked
No one knows
The widest abyss
Two stars
Have managed to cross
And I'm glad
Because there should be no limit
That's what I think
Soulmates are
Whether romantic
Or platonic
Just two stars
Born from the same storm
Who were never taught to let go
When you're born from a storm
You're already an impossible
improbability
So
Nothing is out of reach enough
No formidable landscape
Is unfathomable enough
To force a route around that abyss

When you're born in a storm
You seek whatever shelter you can find
So who cares if it takes a lifetime
To build a bridge
To reconnect
The severed piece of your soul
Clocks do not survive storms
There everything lasts forever
But yet
For that fleeting moment
On that bridge
You understand
That just because you were born into
darkness
Doesn't mean
You'll never see the sun
And it doesn't have to mean
That you're the only one

(maybe they're real, maybe they aren't)

I want to be immortalised
But in the vaguest sense of the word
Richard Siken said it best
Because "I want to tell you my story
Without having to be in it"
I want to be able
To form the words
And set them free
But leave them with no connection to me
I guess I've always liked mysteries
You can't judge what you can't see
You can't ask for evidence
To prove what has never been
But I want to be known
I want someone to look at the stars
And hear my laugh
Or hold a book and feel the weight of my
heart
A misguided collection of recollections
The pieces made to be seen
I don't want to be a painting on a vase
Subjected to the musings of poets' past
But it would be nice if all the stories were
told

It would be nice
If my soul never had to grow old

    (immortality doesn't have to be wilde)

Note to self
Print off the homework for tomorrow
Don't let those 2 hours go to waste

Note to self
Take the dog for a walk
The exercise will do you good

Note to self
Empty the bins
You have time

Note to self
Remember to breathe
Your world doesn't have to end because
theirs does

Note to self
It's ok to start a new chapter
Not everyone should come with you

Note to self
Their choices were not your responsibility
No matter how badly they wanted them to
be

Note to self
Shoulders back
Head up
The only way is forward.

(scattered on my bedroom floor)

I'm both awake and asleep
Isn't that the best thing to be?

(busy building my own world – care to join?)

Lightning Source UK Ltd.
Milton Keynes UK
UKHW020930171122
412303UK00002B/26